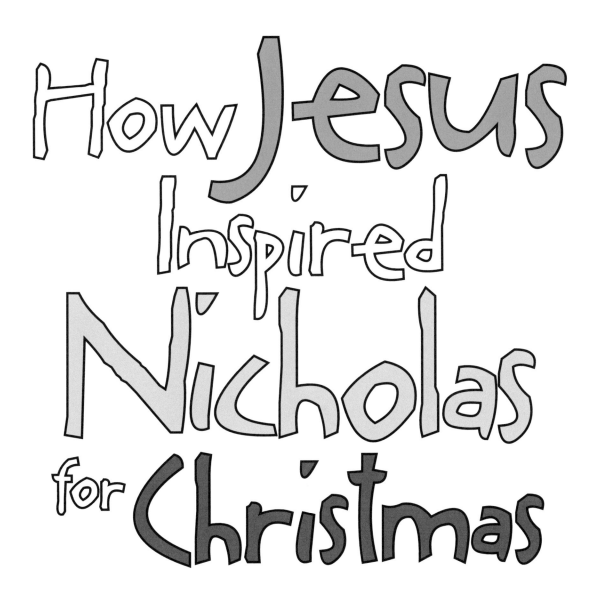

# How Jesus Inspired Nicholas for Christmas

Talee Laurén Auerswald

WestBow Press books may be ordered through booksellers or by contacting:

WestBow Press
A Division of Thomas Nelson & Zondervan
1663 Liberty Drive
Bloomington, IN 47403
www.westbowpress.com
844-714-3454

Because of the dynamic nature of the Internet, any web addresses or links contained in this book may have changed since publication and may no longer be valid. The views expressed in this work are solely those of the author and do not necessarily reflect the views of the publisher, and the publisher hereby disclaims any responsibility for them.

Any people depicted in stock imagery provided by Getty Images are models, and such images are being used for illustrative purposes only.
Certain stock imagery © Getty Images.

ISBN: 978-1-6642-5582-1 (sc)
ISBN: 978-1-6642-5583-8 (e)

Library of Congress Control Number: 2022900991

Print information available on the last page.

WestBow Press rev. date: 7/29/2022

WESTBOW
PRESS®
A DIVISION OF THOMAS NELSON
& ZONDERVAN

# How Jesus Inspired Nicholas for Christmas

Once, there was a man named Nicholas who since being a little boy had an easy time understanding the love and generosity of God's heart.

One night after reading about Jesus' love for children in the Bible, Nicholas had a revelation.

In that moment, he truly understood that every single child on the earth was very important to God.

Nicholas was overcome with compassion. He felt called to provide for children in a new and generous way. Especially, for those children in need.

Nicholas was going to make gifts for children
with the carpenter skills God gave him!

To make sure that God got all the credit for these gifts,
Nicholas decided to keep this all one big secret. Nobody
was going to know that it was him who made them!

So, he sat down and prayed and asked God to give him an increase of creativity and thoughtfulness, so that he'd know exactly what the kids in his community needed. He began creating immediately!

He started working on a few toys that he had in mind.

He made a puzzle for Paul who is
learning how to spell his name.

He made a puzzle for Lydia who is
learning her shapes.

He noticed Leon walked home from school and was always carrying a lot of books, so he made him a wagon.

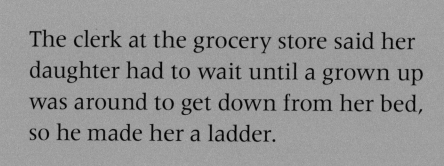

The clerk at the grocery store said her daughter had to wait until a grown up was around to get down from her bed, so he made her a ladder.

Finally, it was the night of December 24<sup>th</sup> and Nicholas had finished all his gifts. In honor of celebrating Jesus' birth, Nicholas decided to deliver the gifts before dawn. That way, the children could wake up to the experience of opening the gifts on Jesus' birthday.

Nicolas was so excited for the children to feel the pure joy of receiving such generosity—just like our Father in heaven was generous when He gave us Jesus.

Because Nicholas lived in a small town where he
knew all the families and loved them very much,
he knew exactly where the children lived!

To keep the families from waking up, he dropped
the presents off on their front yards, under their
trees, and wrapped them to keep them dry.

After Christmas passed, the talk around town was,
"Who gave our kids these amazing and thoughtful gifts?"

Because Nicholas continued this tradition every year at Christmas, the town had no one else to give credit to but Jesus!

Everyone danced and cheered, "Only God could inspire this kind of generosity and love!"

It wasn't until after Nicholas passed away when his son found the journal Nicholas used to design his gifts that his story became known.

You see, Christmas is a celebration of Jesus' birth onto the earth. It is a celebration of the sacrifice and the unconditional love that God has for us, which is shown through the giving of His only son.

Red symbolizes the sacrifice made by an individual to give to the other.

Green represents the new life given to the giver and receiver through this kind act.

Now, we get to experience generosity for ourselves!

This Christmas, ask Jesus to help you be "Santa" to someone in your community.

Remember, they can't know that it's you!

**Merry Christmas!**

Printed in the United States
by Baker & Taylor Publisher Services